Sonnetized
For Your Protection

Selected Poems 1972-2009
Frank Ramirez

Christopher Marlowe & Associates
Everett, Pennsylvania
2009

Orders and inquiries:
Frank Ramirez
1672 Lower Snake Spring Road
Everett PA 15537
(814) 652-2634
ramirez.frank.r@gmail.com

Or through www.createspace.com/3396226

ISBN 1448683734

1st Edition 2009

To Jerry and Marta Lear, with gratitude for a long, happy, and enduring friendship.

"...There's ither poets, much your betters,
Far seen in Greek, deep men o' letters,
Hae thought they had ensur'd their debtors,
              A' future ages:
Now moths deform, in shapeless tatters,
                   Their unknown pages."
              Epistle to James Smith
              – Robert Burns

Juvenilia

Wind song

The song the winds are singing lures
Me on to dreams and distant ways.
I follow. Through a thousand days
It fades at times but it endures.

quatre poèmes

Gently Rotting Sonnet

Crisp leaves clatter on the concrete when they all fall dry
And the arid wind blows.
           The colors fade. The last cow grieves.
The brown corn rustles. I will someday die.
The dust from autumn sheaves
Has settled on the graves of kings and paupers proud,
And birds have long since fled and hoppers turn to wood,
Their joints grinding loud
Where the ants once stood.
And pumpkins sag misshapen, silent, opening to seeds
Which float in clear offal but
               the cold air drowns the stench.
Too late tomatoes fall and greeds
Which planted them in May have all been quenched.
   The winter looms like comfort with a blanket of snow;
   And did I say that I will die? I might have. I think so.

Last, Autumn

Slow the fall of leaves on silent breezes.

Slow the fall as leaves are drained of color and the frost emerges like the lithic walls toyed by Anasazi artists though on the edge of famine.

Slow the fall! Seize moments scattered like the leaves that layer forest floors while Yule is passing into January's bright surrender to the stars no longer distant.

Slow. The fall....

Golden at Sunset

Golden at sunset that mote upon the breeze might have been snow.

Shouts of Blue Men Standing

Oh. Angels breathe. So frost like scattered down
Foretells the knell of autumn and the rise
Of winter death. Anxiety has grown,
The days are short, and settled on the *mise-*
En-scéne are players from the edge
Of *Götterdämerung*. Their challenge rings
Like shouts of blue men standing on the hedge
Of Hadrian. A single warrior sings
Derisively of blood from warmer clime
Where twilight in her courts may barely kiss
The earth in passing. Floundering in time
We bail out the seconds and we miss
The flash of green that heralds sun and war.
Beg ice and snow will lose as long before.

Solstice

Katapandaemonia

The shide in celebration of the spring
Unleashed upon the legions of the moon
The Katapandaemoniacs who wing
Through clear night and cloudy. So. Too soon
The vision of their revels fades and fails
The curtain on our unsubstantial play.
Nobody saved the engine of the nails
Or scrabbled for the relics on the day
The long awaited unexpected word
Who dwelt had died, redonned the body, and
As evidence of all that had occurred
Reduced foundations built on level sand
       To rubble. Let the lesser spirits romp,
       Mere shadows of the coming dance and pomp.

Wa and weal

The shortest day approaches and the region
Of the summer stars is morning, the
Bitter hour ere the dawn when Legion
Throttles all our dreams a borning. Wa
And weal legends gather but not seen
Are any signs of their approach.
Security a chimera I ween,
The goddess of this world, a vain reproach.
But even as the hosts of darkness dance
About the bloodied altars of the heath
The lamb who in obedience the lance
Received and willingly the fatal wreath
Of thorns was crowned withal will yet return
And winter die -- and sun the brighter burn.

Layered lakes and frozen

Bang the drums, drive the dragons forth before
They gnash, devour, crush the mother sun.
The ice has layered lakes and frozen shore.
The night is falling and the day is done.
Fly. Demons who would rule eternal dark
Are casting shadows set in biting stone
And cold.
       ...Who broke the spell and left me stark
And lonely, losing transit words on loan
A little while, falling then aback
Confused, and in no order I discern?
It's not enough to lay them in a stack.
Better to ignore this poesy. Yearn
       And live. For yes, the shortest day has passed.
       The solstice is survived. The first is last.

Heaven cast rebellions

We didn't die. We lived again to tell
Of shortened days -- and nights when fay and shide
In broken dances on the edge of hell
Spread rumors of the triumph of the tree
Of Teutons, flames that spire round
The trunk of ages, burning with the hate
And weight of separation from the sound
Of song celestial, while from glory's gate
The hosts of heaven cast rebellion's crew
As stars that fall like lightning to be dashed
On breakers in the ether. As the few
Who light rejected, then in time were pashed
      Beyond the year's horizon, I can see
      The word made flesh, the spring, and Calvary.

new lamps for old

So long? It wasn't long I put aside
My pen, to seal casements on the walls
Of plotted mats that I would hang beside
The opus pining. Shouting from the stalls
"NEW LAMPS FOR OLD" -- have I a bargain made
That I will soon regret? Who made the rules?
Arrest the night and gather sound and shade
Or shide and wee will gather all the fools.
I long for rest. The best is fairly past.
The pen was dry and thirsty to be filled
Again. The shadows that we cast
Are fading. Snow is falling. All are stilled
And stunned. This matter built on foot and rhyme
Is mine to solve, should I be given time.

sol y sombre

Helicon is cold.

A score of summers walls me from my youth
When pillars aimed at heaven rose in flame,
When at our feet was space and time and truth,
Team-tethered to our will. The roll of fame
Included heroes who in consoled row
Directed Icarus on Babel base
To leap for yokels at a raree show
And safely land. Across the sky a trace
Of glory lingers. Helicon is cold.
Who dares in timid ages to suggest
That once upon a time intrepid, bold,
And brazen pilots, brightest and the best,
      Won honor at the finish of the test
      And lived in touching livid Dian's breast?

Rock Jupiter

Though outwardly the planets (note they pass
Like motes serenely into voided space)
Trace glorias in one eternal mass,
Obeying as about the sun they chase –
Yet inwardly they seethe. The taunting roils
Rock Jupiter with quincentenniel storms.
With fiery breath spouts Io. Venus boils.
And sundered Mimas broods upon her harms.
A blue star, Tellus, high in Ares' dome
Reserves her painted face for suitor eyes
While we, her children, huddled in our home,
Bear witness to bright bolts across the skies.
      So I, obsession's child, must seem kind
      While rack and ruin inward rot my mind.

Stars is rising

The hunter with his belt of triple stars
Is rising with the failing of the age
And free again for having loosed the bars
Of summer, he is potent in his rage.
The seven sisters, lost while sinners baked
In sun and solstice, pushing back the care
And collars that would follow when they raked
The autumn leaves, have reappeared to dare
Us once again with winter and the killing frost.
Who seeks to understand the vertigo
Attendant on the spinning world and lost
Would better marvel that the world is so --
For having got creation as a given,
We living should not wonder at a heaven.

The leaping hare

The sun and moon in tandem heaven flout
And banish night in high or low degree.
A double fortnight calls them around about
To duet dance celestial fantasy.
Through ten and twice a year the solar glare
Obscures the leaping hare of Chinese lore.
Diana is revenged. The huntress' snare
Eclipses glory, evens far the score!
But never equal, never twins the twain.
You marked not nature with those orbs designed
Divinely. Who would choose might choose again
And taste the mirrored pleasure he should find.
    Your words that beg discovery are found
      In Neptune's proud desmene and terraced pond.

Europa's ice and io

Gaunt with age, his features drawn and haggard,
At heaven's gate proud Zeus (who conquered time),
Still languishing from lack of worship, staggered
In his infirmity, admits no crime.
Where once the hills were wont to rock with thunder
When he would deign to step from his domain
Zeus ponders. Who can penetrate the blunder
While all about him falls a quiet rain?
The king is dead. ...not dead? Not while, in passing,
A Voyager should catch a glimpse of gold
And send back from the stars his final blessing
Preserved in fragile pictures in its hold.
  Europa's ice and Io's fiery breath
  With Jupiter fight entropy and death.

Meggido

With martyrs' trophied skulls

Upon the plain of Meggido they gather.
The scimitars are flashing in the sun.
The clouds presage a change is in the weather
And soon the days of conflict will be done.
Prepared in rage to overwhelm the lamb
And his assembled saints from ages called,
To if they may tear tendon, heart and limb,
And burn to bitumen the heaven's walls.
They charge. Is Babylon triumphant,
Her standard raised, her princes grim arrayed,
With martyrs' trophied skulls ascendant,
No end in sight their rule of sun and shade?
      Nay. As the waves are spent against the shore,
      They roil and retreat, are seen no more.

To rotter pits where all

They stamp against the earth that does not yield.
Impatiently they champ against the day
That soon will send them rushing to the field
As armies garbed in red will battle gray.
They wheel and crash amid the bitter fray
As steel set on steel shatters shield
Until the final lurid setting ray
Brings darkness on the weapons that they wield.
Above the bloody din the rocked and reeled
Wan horses paw among the bodies stray.
And fallen riders tossed in wains are wheeled
To rotter pits where all the corpses stay
  Till swords at last are given unto rust
  And clay is fine compounded into dust.

cracked stillness

Silence. The last of the seals is cracked.
Stillness. The hosts with the elders, the law,
And the prophets assembled (the earth below wracked)
Are stunned by the end. As John himself saw
Can anyone look through eternity's glass
And speak any clearer than he who gazed
By the strength of the spirit? It will pass.
The glimpses of glory when love the earth razed
And threw from her orbit the wandering orb
That preconceived notions should prove long agley
And though revelation is tough to absorb,
Its sweet taste and sour suffices to say
In an antediluvian manner and post
That all by his love shall be called to the host.

Shaxpur

In misery we traffic: plagueyear 1592-1593

Full twice twelve month the cockpits coséd are.
No flag unfurléd beckons patrons gay.
We may not trace above a fixéd star.
The clouds have heaven clos'd. No searching ray
Of light will naked cleanse the leprous earth.
Perhaps from Jove a bolt of lightning grim
Would bake and bless where dwells a wicked dearth
Before the memory of plays is dim.
In misery we traffic these few hours
But who in times of devil's pestilence
Will buy these wares? First fall the cleansing showers
And trap this sickness in her little fence,
    For then, when safe, again upon the stage
    We'll tell the tale of this our splendid age.

My sinful province bear (Emilia's sonnet)

A.L Rowse contended that Emilia Lanier was mistress to both William Shakespeare and his patron, Henry Wriothesly, Earl of Southampton, Baron of Titchfield. This would make her the "Dark Lady of the Sonnets." She was herself an accomplished poet.

Like Autumn's promise is my lover bent
Who warm should seek me when I reke it not,
But coldly folds while scarce the day is spent
And I am in the winter fertile caught.
Who steals what I carry marries trash
Which for the well it prospers may it bear
From all my misadventures cupid's rash
To he who would my sinful province share.
But he who in his sugared sonnets sends
Before the eyes of any who should read
A calumny, a false retort that wends
To my report these injuries that bleed
      Should not expect that I his love for lex
      Mistake, but that I will his suiting vex.

Chaco Summer

The memory of stones

The desert wind blows hot and dry
    And scours away the dust
But polishes these ancient stones
    That rest here without rust.

Don't listen. Hear! And Quiet!
    Lizard scuttles in dispute
For precious shade. The old gods bide.
    I hear a distant flute.

The notes are wafting lazily
    Above earth mother's breast
That bakes in place these monuments
    Where humans took their rest.
And if you listen carefully
    As swelling, soft then strong,
Then waning as the twilight dims,
    The flute player plays his song.

Each grain of sand is tumbling,
    And the years they mark are long.
On undiscovered pottery
    The flute player plays his song.

With eyes alone you mark me.
     Do not touch. The dream will shatter
And leave behind your world of flash
     Where nothing much can matter.
The old gods bide in hallowed caves
     Against anointed days,
But you can see them dancing
     In the shimmer of the haze.

Our wasting days are measured,
     Metered on a mitered stick.
But Kronos melts that ruler
     Where the glassy grains are thick.
Your boots are clumsy. Sandaled feet
     Once trod these miles long.
Stand patiently if you would hear
     The flute player and his song.

The earth is waning. Centuries
Of generations strong
Have left no trace that comes to light.
Forever sands away to sight
Are shimmering. Ambition bright
Has given way at last to night.
The flute player plays his song.

Bones of ancient earth

The bones of ancient earth are mixed on mount
And mesa with our native fathers and
Our mothers, who beneath the bowl could count
The stars like brethren infinite as sand.
This bond, this graft of sky and dust
Is still remembered by the winds who howl
Through canyons. Though surrendered to the dust
Are works by later humans, lute and owl
In concert call to mind the stories of our ancestors
Who wandered north to find
This land which like a *madre* they could love
And we will not forget or leave behind
This covenant, whose compact may be seen
At dawn as purple hills turn brown and green.

Womb of dreams

Is this the womb of dreams? The silent witness
Of the stones mask cruelties and kindness
Centuries removed and coded angels
Like a codex counting sun and moon
In step and dance across the heavens
Stays our scant attention at the terminus
Of dusty, unpaved, ribbed and scoured roads.

Here rests the womb of dreams and ours alone
Are left. The dreamers walked to Salmon,
Aztec, and Paquimes, and they woke,
Remembered nothing but the aimless notes
Of flute and drum.

They left their turquoise, left their trash, their troubles,
As well as all who fueled with sinew, muscle, bone,
Whose nights were spent in houses pit on south
And days in wrestling life from drying earth.

They walked a final time the giddy stairs,
Their ceremony keyed to hidden stars.

Like teeth ground to the nerves by corn and sand
These chiseled stones are testimony and…

Star Seeker

In the land of our fathers
Where our mothers still sing,
Rabbit jumped over the star.
Rabbit jumped once and then he jumped twice
But the third time the star was no more.

What We Know

These stones need never speak aloud
Of daughters and their fathers and goodbye
And corn in better years and poorer
And infants slowly laid in teary graves
And shadows lengthened by the children growing.
We know these for a fact though we see nothing.
The human thread unbroken binds us tightly.

Away

i

Mountains like flint
Flaked like arrowheads.
Long forgotten hunters.
The hunter drops his tools

ii

Walk away.
Walk and leave behind the work of hands and heart.
Leave while stars still spin across the sky.
Leave while memory is sharp though wist and wanton.
Walls are tired. Leave while there remains a shred
Of possibility within these rooms.
Leave while there is laughter. Leave with tears.
Burn away the ceilings of the kivas.
Walk away and leave behind the work of hands and
heart.
      Leave behind these riddles in the ruins.

Archaeology

The desert winds blow dry
    And scours away the dust
But polishes adobe
    Ad Memorium sans rust.

Don't listen. Heart! And Hwaet!
    A lizard scuttles in dispute
By precious shade. The old gods bide.
    I hear a distant flue.

The notes are wafting lazily
    Above earth mother's breast
That bakes in place these monuments
    Where [   ] took their rest.
And if you listen carefully
    As swelling [
        ] *scrabbling insect* [
        ] *a bit* [

Each grain of sand is tumbling
    And the years they count are long.
On undiscovered hillsides
    The flute player plays his song.

With eyes alone you mark me.
    Do not touch. The dream will shatter.
And leave behind your [

The waxing days are measured,
     Metered on a mitered stick.
But Kairos melts that measure
     Where the glassy grains [   ]
Your boots are clumsy. Sandaled feet
     Once trod these miles long.
Stand patiently if you would hear
     The flute player plays his song.

The earth is waning [
     ] sands away to sight [

] flute [

On the death of Samuel Beckett

Their merry doom

So *ave atque vale* and farewell.
Two men were standing by a barren path.
They calmly waited on the edge of hell
And chaos, while their author cut a swath
Through silence. Do not ask the meaning of
These moments. What they are is what they is.
A better writer could not order prove.
Like demons cramped upon the plain of Dis
We watch in fascination as the ants
Their merry doom encompass in an hour,
Regardless of what satisfaction wants.
Can anyone deny the brutal power
Of he who wrote of loneliness and stench,
Not naming pain in English and in French?

Nothing looked like something

What did he? Watt in measured patience mulled
The actions of the tuners and reviewed
Their words *ad nauseam* lest he be fooled
Until distilled, and all the pieces glued
Into their parts constituent and still
It made no sense and so he kenned at last
That nothing happened deftly and with skill,
That absence masked as presence clearly passed.
That nothing looked like something. The array
Of incremented incidents plagued Watt
Until the even swallowed up the day
He left the service of abyssal Knott.
With syzygy's mask nothing had occurred.
His passing went unnoticed and unheard.

Old Frog Pond

Old Frog Pond

Old frog pond.
The same frog.
Never the same frog.

Midnight every cat

Midnight. Every cat is black or grey.
The world has stopped and every breath is drawn
With apprehension. Can it be the shee
Are loosed again to run upon the lawn
To tear apart the curtain of the dew?
We shudder as they pass upon the road,
Their steps an echo, every mouth a moue
That sees the goblins bring to life the woad.
A moment and the vision disappears,
And dawn's reprise, to bathe the world in light,
Dispelling and ignoring native fears.
Are wee and tiny bumps within the night
The herald of the imminent return
Of dragons for which all the children yearn?

Antipastoral

As one whose younger days were spent upon
A farm, who early woke to drudgery,
Close to life, yet distant; then, when a man,
Returns, discovers pastorality,
Writes tracts of Shepherds Sage, of Time for Thought,
Of Simple Pleasures, bought with simple wits,
Ignores the blankness simplicity bought,
Forgetting his past, while Work-Weary spits
Upon the dung-doppled pastures of grass
And curses his sheep and curses his farm,
And curses the poet, calls him an ass
(Musings romantic for him have no charm):
  So tend we all to view our distant past.
  We soften the edges and costume the cast.

Orion on a moon

There's a jet knifing through the heart of Orion
On a moon bright night
Banishing the other winter stars.

pandemic i accept

caw you upstart crows wheel against the sky
i know the sun my friend i am a hawk
you gambol in the carrion and mock
while i have seen the true and treasures lie
in rainbow rings on breasts of cloud and sol
a raptured raptor i have soared on wind
that tickled afrik peaks when i have sinned
its pride pandemic i accept the fall
for eden's distant sword aflame has warmed
my wings unmoving every time i climbed
the region of the summer stars unlimed
the trees where liliths bees have haply swarmed

you others know the guts but i as lord
of sky and wind and sea am swift as sword

White snow white

White snow white. White tracks white, rabbit tracks white, white on white, snow on snow.

Clear ice, white powder crushed, crushed white powder, scraped layer, new snow white on white on white.

Falling snow like mist, hard mist, diamond bright cutting, cutting cheeks, white tracks white, rabbit tracks white.

White snow, light snow, piled high, stump high, white snow white.

Winds knife white snow white. Winds knife diamond bright cutting.

White snow white.

Bare trees silver grey, white snow white. Old nests, bare trees, empty nests old nests white snow white. Bare branches, bare twigs, ice clad, bent low, winds knife diamond bright cutting. Clear ice, white powder crushed, crushed white powder, scraped layer, new snow white on white on white. Winds blow, trees low bent so, snow fall. White snow white.

Grey sky, white clouds, unseen sun setting, bare trees silver grey, white snow white. Bare trees, empty nests, old nests, bare twigs, ice clad, bent low, winds knife diamond bright cutting. Sun unseen set. Clouds clear. Ice stars, diamond bright cutting. White snow white.

Black birds fluttering, black birds lighting, bare trees, silver grey, white snow white.

Wind wipe clouds away. Greek moon rising, bright white, blue long shadows, white show white, unseen sun set, bare trees silver grey, diamond bright cutting shatters Greek moon light, white snow white.

White tracks white, rabbit tracks white, rabbit long gone, Greek moon shone, blue long shadows, clear ice, white powder crushed, crushed white powder, scraped layer, new snow white on white on white.

Last snows fall, rabbit long gone, rabbit tracks gone, Greek moon shone, blue long shadows, bare trees silver grey, white snow white. Old nests, bare trees, empty nests old nests white snow white. Bare branches, bare twigs, ice clad, bent low, winds knife diamond bright cutting. Clear ice, white powder crushed, crushed white powder, scraped layer, new snow white on white on white. Winds blow, trees low bent so, snow fall. My tracks gone.

White snow white.

Canvas Adam's sons

These rocks are church. This ground around is holy.
Their history divine, though grey, is read.
By those who humbly pass and honor solely
The one who pasteled stone. In silent dread.

Don't chip. Don't mar. Don't gather for tomorrow.
Devour what you can with eye and ear
And taste the air this day and do not borrow
Against what you may never earn nor fear.

And while you stare in wonder at the waters
Look all about you at the host who share
This canvas. Adam's sons and Eve's own daughters
Who in their time God's burden each can bear,

Creating in each heart or in a few
The image of the maker and anew.

convoy

If you think that mosquitoes from MI
Are at all on our side then please WI.
Like a trash-laden barge
They're ungainly and large.
When your veins are bled dry they'll just FI.

Orisons

Sonnet

The ark is beached. We do not choose to find
Its crumbling planks upon the mountain's face.
Allow us, Lord, to share the chalice lined
With joyful sorrows from Ignatius' race.
The plain abandoned by the conflict past
Exists. What need to stand upon that dust?
Why visit Patmos when the first and last
Commands us now to act? Let gather rust
The harbored ships of war. We fill the cup
And live the words he spoke upon that hill.
As humble servant, Love commands we sup.
The ancient truth he shared invites us still.
      A life surrendered, then returned in full,
      We count the cost and then become his will.

The night is barely cool

Lord, give me strength. The night is barely cool.
The heart of darkness' reign is still ahead
Though kindness shields us from nature's duel
When sun shall battle shade and take her stead.
The list of tasks is laden with the trite
And I will labor with the necessary.
Forgive me if, with solid work in sight
I sigh for every time my plans miscarry.
For though you set your royal stars ablaze
And every orb is by your power moved
No sparrow falls unnoticed by your gaze.
Each hair is counted, every human loved.
      No love so large it could not find me too,
      No task too small for me to do for you.

Bend and kneel and eye

Leaf fall -- surrender to the call of sleep
And sleep to death, no dreaming, ground below
The tread of those too weary now to keep
The cold from killing. Who dreads to mark the snow?
Blow wind. A mind is wracked with thoughts of doom
And dawn is distant and the king of earth
And morning is still absent from the room
And vault of heaven. Gold is little worth,
Dull is silver, gone are gems' appeal.
I sinned iwis -- why are you distant, Lord?
Resolve my heart, though knee should bend to kneel
And eye be comforted with written word,
And ear and hymn by voices, raised in song,
Be fed until this shattered will is strong.

Personal Archaeology

Snoring dog

Snoring dog, you hog the couch
And leave no room for napping kitty.
When you wake you are no slouch
In repose you're sitting pretty.
Demonstrate to carp that diem
May not mean you have to see 'em
Showing signs of striking motion.
In your slumber is an ocean
Of deep dreaming without potion.

Twitching, moaning, gasp, your eye
Is still moving rapidly.
When you wake should someone sigh.
You're not touched by what you see
In lost Nemo's fantasy.
It's as if your dreams are shed
When your need for sleep is dead.
Though you growl while you are sleeping
There's no grudges in your keeping.
Arise and sheepishly admit
Me to your fellowship and sit.

On first reading Homer's Iliad

Some wonder if Homer wrote Iliad.
Say no if you want to but still he had.
The rage of Achilles
And all those Greek sillies
Could have used some embalming from Gilead.

The leaves in layers

I watch you grow and you are more than you.
There is an other growing, showing more
Each morning, and the hope a borning due
Allows us to release upon the shore
Of time our burdens. Watch the baby walk
In mind's eye first, who bursts before our eyes.
Reality,! Incarnate, dreams from talk
Through action and surrender will arise.
The leaves in layers sheltered by the years
Will clothe the roots and gnarls. Trees are shod
By memories of auld autumnal fears
And vernally they rediscover God.
      Nativity capitulates in love
      The unforgotten promise from above.

Kirk by sundry

I mauna ardor pen in ither tongue
And I a coof for a' tha'. Here aboon
The struggle wha' maun mak' tha' courtin' lang.
Tho' she I praise alas is claimed eftsoon.
The tower bricked by Nimrod scratched the sky
But words, the blocks which founded the endeavor
Were sundered, and the Babble gave the lie
That we by works may triumph for forever.
So can I hope in any language shared
By cretin and by creeper of the globe
To cull your love, which long before was snared
Or watch at least the rising of the robe?
      No words suffice when words were spoken then.
      Twas witnessed in a kirk I canna ken.

Le roy est mort

We laugh at others' love and think it sport
To watch them caper vain for other eyes.
But are they fools? Too soon *le roy est mort*
And shades envelope simple birth and wise.
The days grow shorter. Summer glads to fade.
The autumn beckons, birds in flight of course.
The memory of plumage gay arrayed
The songs that followed, dying in a corse.
Then let us share the game while time we may.
The more fools they who will not stoop to this --
Embrace as lover every given day
And pride release so we may passion kiss.
      Did autumn call? It came. The year is old.
      We huddle two as one against the cold.

The figure of Beátrice

Is this the time to reexamine my
Obsession? When I call again to mind
The figure of Beátrice and I sigh
"Objection. . . " will my pleas to heaven find
An open door? Excuses. For I mean
To put aside Inferno for a time
And dwell upon her shadow on the green
Until I hear the welling of the chime,
To wait like Constantine until the end;
To hope, upon the edge of gaping hell,
To buy, with flowing tears that I will send,
A Heaven, that my soul might yet be well;
But in despite of knowledge put this off
And sleepily indulge this warning cough.

Epicycles in the feign *(for Jennie)*

No rosebud is eternal but my love
Abides beyond the passage of the sun
Across the signs that on the heavens run
In endless circles, while the planets wove

Strange epicycles in the feigned ellipse
Their paths describe upon the ether's face.
Let falling stars their torch without a trace
Extinguish. Selah. Nothing can eclipse

This love undimmed. So at the end of many years
Recall how young we were and how we ran
Away from cautions, laughed at others' fears
And dared to finish what we first began,

In love and loving passionate and brash.
How bright our fire burns and leaves no ash.

Mittelmarch

Reticentaur

Once long ago in far uncharted lands
A Centaur bold stood, pawed the earth, and mulled.
I stood unawed, for Kronos' measured sands
Had found me young, and still a fool, and fooled.

"Halloo!" I cried. "What news from pale hills?
The Ents in Dudgeon Leaf -- do they meet yet?"
He took no notice of this test of wills,
But godlike grazed, his features firmly set.

"What words from worlds forgotten have your ears
In quiet meditation chanced upon?
What thoughts of wisdom planted by the years
Entwine your revelation couched in song?"

He took no need. "Halloo!" I cried again.
"Am I to be ignored?" I asked with pique.
"I've asked you questions five, must I ask ten
Before you deign," I added barbs, "to speak?"

The manbeast paused, then gripped an oldman tree
And grunting, pulled. I saw its rootage give.
I watched with fear. His gaze was set on me.
He saw my terror, shrugged, and let me live.

Horse and leaf and field

The Pellenor is overrun by foes
Who antlike swarm upon the plain of war.
The remnant of the west which, in the throes
Of black despair, protects the Pellenor,
Have huddled in the Tower of the Guard.
Will riders from the province of the north
(Though adamant the gates they cannot ward)
In time from hasty muster, riding forth
Redeem the pledge before the fatal dawn?
The hungry eye has struck and he whose fief
Is terror from the city has withdrawn
To fall upon the king of horse and leaf
And field, he whom no man mauna slay.
So grim the situation of the day.

Lord of ring and sight

And all the time the only hope of all
Who dwell beneath the memory of light
Of Earendil -- who must not faint or fall ---
Is hidden from the Lord of Ring and sight.
The eye is gazing at the trinket king
Who from the ancient city sallies forth.
His sovereignty the heavens loudly sing.
A feint, a faint distraction. Was it worth
It all to risk the world upon a throw?
Was reason fled in his despite to send
To Sauron's choked domain? The wise should know
But who could have foreseen the bitter end
When he -- the stone rejected -- should redeem
In total all the world, or so I deem.

The Eldar children

The Eldar children first beheld the stars
And loved the night that stretched across the years
Unmeasured. In despite of Morgoth's scars
They treasure still the scattered stellar tears
On moonless nights. Their immortality
Permitted vistas of unnumbered phase.
Should love lie fallow for a century
In confidence resume in latter days.
We have no bounty of incessant tides.
Too soon the seasons grind our paltry shift.
And yet in Wisdom mortal hope abides.
This paucity of days is heaven's gift.
> More precious are our days for we have few.
> And bless so each one I spend with you.

The mariner of night

No will of mine the parting at days' end,
The quiet resignation of repair,
And in despite of conscience I may spend
Another morning and I find you there.
I stand upon the cliffs against the sea
And spot against horizon's haze your sail.
Your course is set. It is not set for me.
Against the drawn ecliptic daylight fails.
But pausing in the embers of the day
The Mariner of Night who knows no port
In Middle Earth, but found the needed way
And tells me day will come and night is short
       And day brings hope. For what I cannot guess.
       I stand alone and watch the sail pass.

The garden is abandoned

Whanne in April -- "Arthur is gone," men cried
In darkness. "...I'm back," he said. The tales
Told by human muses may be haunting
But someone told a better story. Listen:
      Be light! Become! First spoke Agape's word
      Above primeval beasts named Void and Deep.
      A world, conceived and birthed in Clarity
      Was sundered and entombed by serpent/flood.
Creation's glass, where once God could be heard
Through grasses as he walked among us his own,
Was marred by human sin, and dimly seen
Was God's abiding love in pale reflection.
      He who our parents knew once face to face
      Became the voice of thunder and I AM
      Not by God's will but ours. It took a Word
      That bled to call us back and seek his love.
Look closely at this face and touch the wounds
For here's the glass that finally restores
Our vision. God is seen. The Father's son
Rewrote the ending of the devil's song.
      The garden is abandoned. Yet we wander
      Further from the plot claimed by the Adverse,
      For deeper than the rhythms of the sea
      Or songs of sylvan winds above the fields,

Is writ the heart's true wish: Jerusalem,
Still to be purged with us and made anew,
God's city. The spiraled topochronicon
Will be dissolved and Clarity restored.
        EA. So be. The music has begun
        Whose author's name is Judge, and we shall sing
        Our part the clearer if we seek to mirror
        In every note the love that called us forth.

Echo's Bones

In Memoriam

There's a cat-sized hole in the universe and that's why
it's so hard to breathe.

Retreat and you were there

Goodnight sweet gentle thing of fire,
Burn bright in spite of darkness all around.
You seemed as light as autumn leaves that gyre
In wistful circles till they touch the ground.

Ha! That was fair illusion, for like steel
You bent a bit but straightaway the true
Was measured by your metric, which was real,
And was revealed to more than just a few.

Let winter winds and summer heat both batter.
The seasons would retreat, and you were there,
Survivor, for the things you knew that matter
Eternal grace the earth we briefly share.

Too few the years, recedes the ocean foam,
Too great the grace that called to rest and home.

Morning

Still, still, still
Clock stop
Time stall
Still, still, still.

Still, still, still,
Dark calm
Sharp stars
Still, still, still.

Still, still, still
Damp earth
Last leaves
Still, still, still.

Still, still, still,
Empty box
Distant pyre
Embers from
That aging fire
Sparks rise
Spire higher
Still, still, still.

Silky bone and meal

For now I think of how my clay compounded
Into a box of silky bone and meal
Shall be – when all the words have been profounded
And obsequies observed for common weal –

Released unto the rapid running river
The flows beneath the gaze of silent stone
Where native runner found the acorn giver
Of flour. Let the Ansel Adams moon

Rise briefly on my dust while there is churning
In whirls and whorls beyond Yosemite.
This thought has gladly satisfied my yearning
While here upon the earth I am still me.

As for once the thing shall happen – will I care?
You may dump the dust or body anywhere.

Empty cup *kenosis*

The last long drink, the final pouring out of summer,
The first few flakes, the sudden storm that wipes away
the barren trees in winter white
The fading fall that dampens out at last the fitful
                                                    drummer
The failing heart that beats no more as falls eternal night
We thought of nothing
These greying black and white photos
And nothing
And stops and starts and love

One and zero and zero and one
Rise like sparks from greedy fire
Crackling stacks of crumbling logs
Ezekiel saw the zero way in the middle of the air
Dun the byre and newborn pyre
Way in the middle of the air.

Virus

Is there a malediction
Waiting to be incanted
Drawing out malefactors
And prisoning in a prism
Zeroes and ones and zeroes
In a tangle of virus writers
Letting the white light pierce them
And leaving us undisturbed?

Is there a benediction
Waiting to be a blessing,
A balm or a medication
To send to a blessed peace
Zeroes and ones and zeroes
Twisted beyond recognition
Healed to our satisfaction
Given a lasting peace?

What in the end is lasting,
Stretching beyond generations
With messages of condolence
Rhythm and bane and pain
Zeroes and ones and zeroes
Written on parchment paper
Scratched into walls and counters
Voicing our silent prayers?

Cremains to rivers race

The footfalls fade and with the echoes, shade
The long departure of the dusk. The night
Is fast. The dark will wait. The dawn evade
The clock until the land returns to sight.
No trace remains. Cremains to rivers race
And scatter till the waters of the world
In equal measure Neptune's pleasure trace
The capillaries, channels oceans swirled.
Let matter scatter, lest the patter of
The rain too soon to mind the pain recall,
And laughter sculpt the rafter and the love
And all the while smile and mark the fall
Of leaves in measured layers and they err
In death. And silence swallows all I fear.

Dante at the livid step

Beati Pauperes Spiritu!
Purgatorio, XII, 110

Too full of Italy are you, Dante.
You reek and reck too much of Rome,
Said Odysseus before the livid step.
Bruised and purple the faces as well of the long travelers
Who stared face to face, recognizing in an instant
The unrecognizable features in each other.

One P, one Π,
Remains to each. Impatiently the angel hovers,
Anxious that these two should be gone.

My name is not Ulysses, Dante.
Not in Latin but in Greek I spoke
When underneath the glutton sun I cast a shadow,
And since those days the children fair and dark alike
Grew to dance upon the bright and tawny hills
And never knew that either of us stood upon
The ancient earth of story. Theirs the world,
And now that world is dying too.

Are you surprised to see me here?
You never read in Greek my exploits
But were content to damn me for the sin
Of my Achaean birth.

Rome was not all history's end. Don't start.
Nor all Achaia's scattered cities — lights
Upon a thousand hills, united in their
Quest for serpent glory, but only the
One God. Just as each Christian, Jew, and Muslim
Proclaims the Only God, the aim and goal of
Every act and action.

The poet's back was aching still from heavy stones
In circles carried centuries while pride was pried
From Priam's champion.

Still proud? Then know I speared my love,
I captured my Beatrice and not from far her lover sworn
And captured her again amidst the bloody bower of her
wooers,
Spitted fair by spear and arrow flying.

Think you the first to love his native land?
Here never native land is won.

Your fables told, the pit of fire you placed me in — all lies.
Black death awaited — yet I never tasted woe.
Whatever angel told you of our voyage past the teeth
Of Europe never spoke of how the winged boat swirled
And twirled around the whirlpool, so that the Messenger
Plucked every son of Thebes before the boat sank down
to Acheron.

You'll nothing say?
You said I chose one final journey
Within the sight of the giant mountain
But we were not swallowed in the pit.
We were swept ashore to climb Mount Purgatory.

This door is for us twain. Not singly shall we pass
The one without the other.

It is our fate, *amicus*, to walk these steps together
Through liquid glass, the final barrier before
The Holy Mountain and the Wholly Other.
For these many years I've waited while
You flogged yourself beyond the wish
Of gods and angels.

For years your steps re-echoed all alone
Along the track while wrestling with your weight,
The angel marking time until you raised your
Eyes in wonder. Where had all the sinners gone
You asked? Were there others still unpacking
At the shore while Cato glowered? No.
Marzia and he — do not blanche —
Had long abandoned what had been his post
And clambered up and out, long past you
Though you hadn't noticed! –
And why I here? I could have gone
But I your final trial stand and stare you down
And will you turn and clamber down
Before you'd cross the bar with me?

Come, let us meet the true Beatrice together.

Or will you stay, defying earth and heaven for your
Rome,
And ignore your precious Christ, miss your adversaries'
look of shock and awe,
Nor ever gaze upon the endless heavens rife with stars?

Notes

Dante's cosmology circled around Roman and Italian
history. To his way of thinking Troy was a disaster
redeemed by the journey of Aeneas and the founding of
Rome. Well versed in Latin and the Italian vernacular, he
almost certainly did not read the Greek poets in their
original language. Each of the three sections of his
Comedy ended with the word 'stars.'

Dante meets Odysseus on the final steps of purgatory
outside the Earthly Paradise. He knew from his earlier
experience that everyone, regardless of how sinless their
life, must walk through the wall of the fire of molten
glass.

Beati Pauperes Spiritu! "Blessed are the poor in spirit."
This particular beatitude is sung by the Angel of
Humility once the pride-filled soul is purified and
advances from the First to the Second Cornice in
Purgatory.

Dante fully expected that he would spend a
good deal of time in this circle, bent over at the waist
bearing a large stone weight on his back, purging himself
of his besetting sin.

Ulysses. Dante insisted on using the Latin names for the
Greek heroes of Troy. He seems to have resented the
Achaians victory over the Trojans.

Beatrice. Dante glimpsed the beloved Beatrice only twice
in his earthly life. Odysseus reclaimed his wife Penelope
in the midst of great riot and slaughter.

Giant mountain. Dante invented a final voyage for
Odysseus that sent him into the Southern Hemisphere
where in sight of the mountain of Purgatory he and his
crew were caught in a whirlpool. The mariner was
drowned and consigned to the eighth circle of hell for his
supposed sins as an evil counselor. (*Inferno* xxvi)

Cato and Marzia. In the *Comedy* Cato, who committed
suicide rather than submit to the new regime of Julius
Caesar, is not consigned to hell but serves as the pagan
guard of Purgatory. Cato claims he cannot be influenced
by his lover Marzia, who sighs in Limbo with other
ancient pagans who never knew Christ.

**To W. S. Merwyn and the memory of John Ciardi,
translators of the Purgatorio.**

Wen that mars

Are you bewildered? Bid the cast dissolve
As elementals to the dewy air,
Their particles constituent resolve.
Those pennants flapping bravely. Au contraire,
Are not the props of kings but actors' toys
And we, who wrestle with reluctant pen,
Must be the author of the pyrrhic joys.
That much know certain. Mark the fatal wen
That mars our features. What are we to do?
We are the stuff of dreams and nothing claim
Past entertaining. Oy! My play is through.
I must accede -- to praise his holy name.
Enough another year should sail by,
An' still nae kintra ken, though I may try.

L'envoi

612

Afterwards the dawn gives way
To morning. Fingers on the strings
Blend sight and science, greet the day
With gladborn music couched in rings
Of wisdom.

About the author

Ahora mi familia son del mundo.
Un corazon tenemos -- cantare
Lo mismo canto del amor profundo
De los angeles que dice, "Alabare."
The winds that blessed our shorelines south and north
Were like a guide that prodded in all weather,
And past all obstacles has sent us forth,
So now we stand one family together.
        Y las estrellas cerca del cielo
        Like sugar scattered sweetly on our souls
        Are steadfast sentries of the love eternal,
        Recuerdos del viajes mas normal
Porque we come to tie the knot *aqui*,
Casados con Dios, so now we're "we."

Do it yourself kit

It is not hard to write a pretty sonnet.
Just push iambic lambs around,
& £ & £ & £ & £ & £.
These verses wear a rather fetching bonnet.

Stay up to date with everything Shakespearean
& £ & £ & £ & £ & £.
Just push iambic gamboling lambs around.
Some are ethereal and atmospherian.

The rest are like that vapid summer's day.
& £ & £ & £ & £ & £.
Just push iambic rambling lambs around.
But make sure none get lost along the way

And unlike tabloid magazine quintuplets
A sonnet ends content in kipling couplets